The Royal P
in Brussels

Irene Smets

THE ROYAL PALACE IN BRUSSELS

Ludion

The Royal Palace was first opened to the public in 1965, to mark the centenary of the death of King Leopold I. The event drew a great deal of interest, and prompted the Palace to open its doors every year during the summer holidays.

The Royal Palace is located on Coudenberg Hill, the site of the old Palace of the Dukes of Brabant, which was destroyed by fire in 1731. The palace was not replaced immediately but in the final quarter of the 18th century – during the period of Austrian rule – a new district was built there in the neo-classical style. In 1815, two buildings from that period were selected as the residence of King William I of the Netherlands and duly altered. So Brussels once again had a royal residence. King Leopold I inherited a palace that was still covered in scaffolding. It was only at the very end of his reign, however, that he let his son draw up plans to extend the building and asked the government's permission to go ahead with the necessary works. The rooms the public sees today date from one of these three stages of construction.

Visitors can also admire the varied and valuable collection of art with which the Palace is decorated. The Royal Collection ranges from a small vase in Brussels porcelain, to an Empire chair with exceptionally attractive Beauvais tapestrywork or a state portrait of King Leopold I.

Nevertheless, the Palace is not a museum. When the summer holidays are over and the doors close once again, 'normal' life returns, with a succession of audiences, working meetings, receptions and official events. Providing the public with an insight into the King's working environment makes a modest contribution towards a better understanding of our constitutional system and to a greater sense of identity between the people and the government. The initiative is primarily aimed, therefore, at people living in Belgium, of whatever background. On the other hand, the summer is the most popular time for foreign visitors to come to Belgium and to Brussels, and so the Royal Palace offers a warm welcome to all its visitors.

p. 2 Hall of Mirrors with Jan Fabre's decorated ceiling (see p. 60)

Monogram of King Leopold II and Queen Marie-Henriette, corner motif in the parquet floor of the Long Gallery

The Grand Marshal of the Court

The Royal Palace is the King's official residence. It is here that he receives his ministers and advisers, ambassadors and guests. And it is here too that he deals with the affairs of state. The Royal Household, which helps the King to perform his duties, has its offices here. This fine palace is, therefore, both a working and a meeting place. It is open to the public for several weeks every year.

The setting in which these activities take place is, however, far from everyday. The Palace still appears largely as it did in the 19th and early 20th centuries, following the alterations, extensions and refurbishment carried out under William I of the Netherlands and Leopold II. The drawing rooms have, of course, been adapted in the ensuing years, but only to a limited extent. Much of the furniture and many of the ornaments and works of art remain in their original places.

It is precisely because this is still a working building that great care is taken to maintain it. Major restoration work was carried out, for instance, between 1985 and 1990, throughout which the utmost attention was paid to maintaining the building's authenticity. Since 2002, the Palace has also incorporated work by contemporary artists.

All of this makes the Palace an exceptional place. It is a living building, in which every room, piece of furniture and work of art has its own history – and one that is far from complete.

Grand Staircase, central dome (see p. 36)

After centuries of foreign rule, Belgians declared their independence in September 1830. They appointed a National Congress as their temporary government, which set to work immediately on drafting a new constitution and selecting a suitable monarch. The Belgian throne was duly offered to Prince Leopold of Saxe-Coburg. On 21 July 1831 he took the oath laid out in the new constitution and was crowned King Leopold I of the Belgians. The same oath has since been sworn by all his successors:

'I swear that I shall uphold the constitution and laws of the Belgian people, that I shall maintain the nation's independence and preserve its territorial integrity.'

Since 1890, 21 July – the anniversary of the first coronation – has been celebrated as Belgium's National Day.

King Albert II, Queen Paola, Prince Philippe and Princess Mathilde in the Throne Room during the New Year reception for the government on 25 January 2000

Ary Scheffer, *King Leopold I*, 1838, oil on canvas.
Ceremonial Vestibule

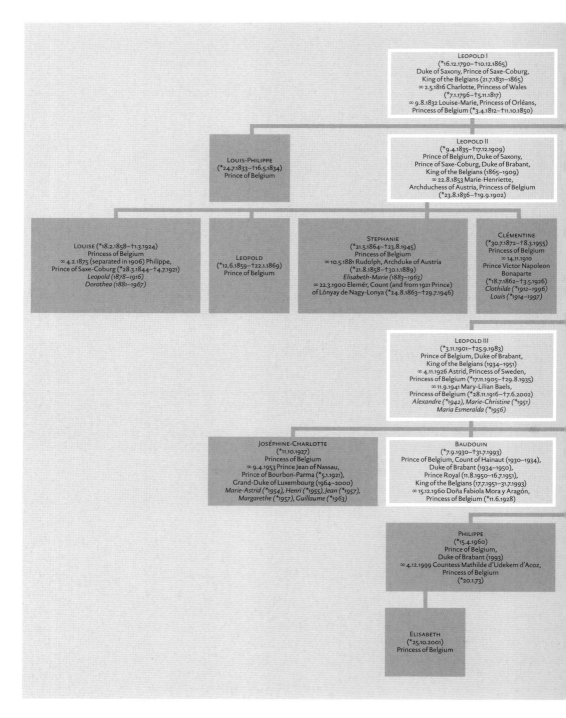

LEOPOLD I
(*16.12.1790–†10.12.1865)
Duke of Saxony, Prince of Saxe-Coburg,
King of the Belgians (21.7.1831–1865)
∞ 2.5.1816 Charlotte, Princess of Wales
(*7.1.1796–†5.11.1817)
∞ 9.8.1832 Louise-Marie, Princess of Orléans,
Princess of Belgium (*3.4.1812–†11.10.1850)

LOUIS-PHILIPPE
(*24.7.1833–†16.5.1834)
Prince of Belgium

LEOPOLD II
(*9.4.1835–†17.12.1909)
Prince of Belgium, Duke of Saxony,
Prince of Saxe-Coburg, Duke of Brabant,
King of the Belgians (1865–1909)
∞ 22.8.1853 Marie-Henriette,
Archduchess of Austria, Princess of Belgium
(*23.8.1836–†19.9.1902)

LOUISE (*18.2.1858–†1.3.1924)
Princess of Belgium
∞ 4.2.1875 (separated in 1906) Philippe,
Prince of Saxe-Coburg (*28.3.1844–†4.7.1921)
Leopold (1878–1916)
Dorothea (1881–1967)

LEOPOLD
(*12.6.1859–†22.1.1869)
Prince of Belgium

STEPHANIE
(*21.5.1864–†23.8.1945)
Princess of Belgium
∞ 10.5.1881 Rudolph, Archduke of Austria
(*21.8.1858–†30.1.1889)
Elisabeth-Marie (1883–1963)
∞ 22.3.1900 Elemér, Count (and from 1921 Prince)
of Lónyay de Nagy-Lonya (*24.8.1863–†29.7.1946)

CLÉMENTINE
(*30.7.1872–†8.3.1955)
Princess of Belgium
∞ 14.11.1910
Prince Victor Napoleon
Bonaparte
(*18.7.1862–†3.5.1926)
Clothilde (*1912–1996)
Louis (*1914–1997)

LEOPOLD III
(*3.11.1901–†25.9.1983)
Prince of Belgium, Duke of Brabant,
King of the Belgians (1934–1951)
∞ 4.11.1926 Astrid, Princess of Sweden,
Princess of Belgium (*17.11.1905–†29.8.1935)
∞ 11.9.1941 Mary-Lilian Baels,
Princess of Belgium (*28.11.1916–†7.6.2002)
Alexandre (*1942), Marie-Christine (*1951)
Maria Esmeralda (*1956)

JOSÉPHINE-CHARLOTTE
(*11.10.1927)
Princess of Belgium
∞ 9.4.1953 Prince Jean of Nassau,
Prince of Bourbon-Parma (*5.1.1921),
Grand-Duke of Luxembourg (1964–2000)
Marie-Astrid (*1954), Henri (*1955), Jean (*1957),
Margarethe (*1957), Guillaume (*1963)

BAUDOUIN
(*7.9.1930–†31.7.1993)
Prince of Belgium, Count of Hainaut (1930–1934),
Duke of Brabant (1934–1950),
Prince Royal (11.8.1950–16.7.1951),
King of the Belgians (17.7.1951–31.7.1993)
∞ 15.12.1960 Doña Fabiola Mora y Aragón,
Princess of Belgium (*11.6.1928)

PHILIPPE
(*15.4.1960)
Prince of Belgium,
Duke of Brabant (1993)
∞ 4.12.1999 Countess Mathilde d'Udekem d'Acoz,
Princess of Belgium
(*20.1.73)

ELISABETH
(*25.10.2001)
Princess of Belgium

Genealogy
of the Belgian Royal Family

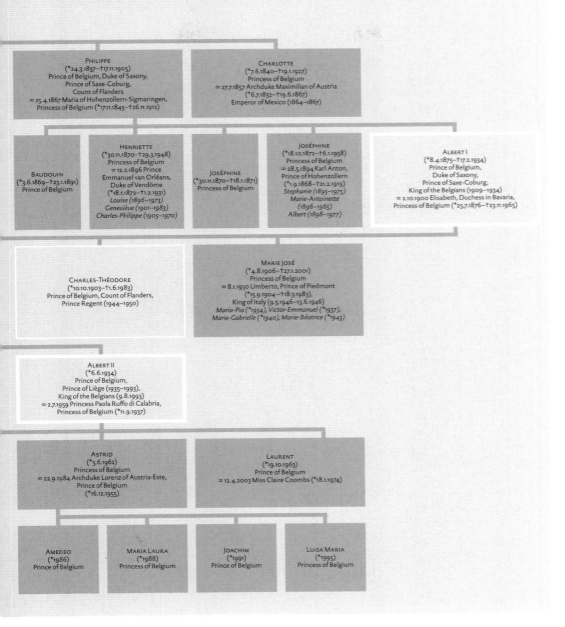

PHILIPPE
(*24.3.1837–†17.11.1905)
Prince of Belgium, Duke of Saxony,
Prince of Saxe-Coburg,
Count of Flanders
∞ 25.4.1867 Maria of Hohenzollern-Sigmaringen,
Princess of Belgium (*17.11.1845–†26.11.1912)

CHARLOTTE
(*7.6.1840–†19.1.1927)
Princess of Belgium
∞ 27.7.1857 Archduke Maximilian of Austria
(*6.7.1832–†19.6.1867)
Emperor of Mexico (1864–1867)

BAUDOUIN
(*3.6.1869–†23.1.1891)
Prince of Belgium

HENRIETTE
(*30.11.1870–†29.3.1948)
Princess of Belgium
∞ 12.2.1896 Prince
Emmanuel van Orléans,
Duke of Vendôme
(*18.1.1872–†1.2.1931)
*Louise (1896–1973)
Geneviève (1901–1983)
Charles-Philippe (1905–1970)*

JOSÉPHINE
(*30.11.1870–†18.1.1871)
Princess of Belgium

JOSÉPHINE
(*18.10.1872–†6.1.1958)
Princess of Belgium
∞ 28.5.1894 Karl Anton,
Prince of Hohenzollern
(*1.9.1868–†21.2.1919)
*Stephanie (1895–1975)
Marie-Antoinette
(1896–1965)
Albert (1898–1977)*

ALBERT I
(*8.4.1875–†17.2.1934)
Prince of Belgium,
Duke of Saxony,
Prince of Saxe-Coburg,
King of the Belgians (1909–1934)
∞ 2.10.1900 Elisabeth, Duchess in Bavaria,
Princess of Belgium (*25.7.1876–†23.11.1965)

CHARLES-THÉODORE
(*10.10.1903–†1.6.1983)
Prince of Belgium, Count of Flanders,
Prince Regent (1944–1950)

MARIE JOSÉ
(*4.8.1906–†27.1.2001)
Princess of Belgium
∞ 8.1.1930 Umberto, Prince of Piedmont
(*15.9.1904–†18.3.1983),
King of Italy (9.5.1946–13.6.1946)
*Maria-Pia (*1934), Victor-Emmanuel (*1937),
Marie-Gabrielle (*1940), Marie-Béatrice (*1943)*

ALBERT II
(*6.6.1934)
Prince of Belgium,
Prince of Liège (1935–1993),
King of the Belgians (9.8.1993)
∞ 2.7.1959 Princess Paola Ruffo di Calabria,
Princess of Belgium (*11.9.1937)

ASTRID
(*5.6.1962)
Princess of Belgium
∞ 22.9.1984 Archduke Lorenz of Austria-Este,
Prince of Belgium
(*16.12.1955)

LAURENT
(*19.10.1963)
Prince of Belgium
∞ 12.4.2003 Miss Claire Coombs (*18.1.1974)

AMEDEO
(*1986)
Prince of Belgium

MARIA LAURA
(*1988)
Princess of Belgium

JOACHIM
(*1991)
Prince of Belgium

LUISA MARIA
(*1995)
Princess of Belgium

LEOPOLD I,
KING FROM 1831 TO 1865

King Leopold I was the ideal person to defend the young Belgium's right to exist among Europe's then Great Powers. He was of German descent, while as the widower of Princess Charlotte of Wales, he could rely on the support of Great Britain. He also enjoyed good relations with the Tsar of Russia, on whose side he had fought against Napoleon. And thanks to his marriage to the French Princess Louise-Marie of Orléans, France, too, was favourably disposed to his new kingdom.

Apart from being well connected, Leopold also had the right qualities. As a general in the Russian army, he had gained valuable military experience. He also developed his diplomatic skills while negotiating on behalf of the Duchy of Saxe-Coburg with the Great Powers, which wished to redraw the map of Europe following the defeat of Napoleon at Waterloo. And he was an effective tactician, too, with a good grasp of how internal affairs, international relations and the defence of the realm were all intimately connected.

Leopold's aim was to ensure Belgium's viability as an independent nation. With that goal in mind, he promoted trade and the country's nascent industry, and displayed a great interest in the building of the first railway in continental Europe – the Brussels-Mechelen line, which opened in 1835.

Copy after Franz-Xaver Winterhalter,
King Leopold I, originally painted in 1843,
oil on canvas. Large White Drawing Room

Queen Louise-Marie

In 1832 Leopold I married Princess Louise-Marie of Orléans, daughter of King Louis-Philippe of France. Although political considerations lay behind their match, the couple went on to enjoy a harmonious marriage. The Queen worked behind the scenes to improve political relations between France and Great Britain, strengthening Belgium's position in the process. She was a generous woman who supported a variety of social causes. Queen Louise-Marie also had a lively interest in art and painted a number of fine watercolours.

Copy after Claude-Marie Dubufe,
Queen Louise-Marie, c. 1836, oil on canvas.
Large White Drawing Room

LEOPOLD II,
KING FROM 1865 TO 1909

King Leopold II had grandiose dreams for his country. He wanted to turn Belgium into an attractive, prosperous, strong and peaceful nation. He spent his time as Duke of Brabant considering how he could achieve his ambitions and, having ascended to the throne, he worked hard to put his plans into practice. He identified town-planning and architecture as means of beautifying the country. Leopold's vision was given concrete form in the development of Brussels, Ostend and Tervueren. And it was under his influence that the Royal Palace assumed its current appearance.

The colonization of the Congo and trade missions to China were part of the King's plan to stimulate Belgium's economic expansion. As tensions rose in Europe in the period around 1870, Leopold became convinced that the country needed a strong army. Shortly before his death, he signed legislation introducing military service.

Nicaise de Keyser, *Prince Leopold, Duke of Brabant (Leopold II)*, 1853, oil on canvas. Ceremonial Vestibule

As a young woman, Marie-Henriette was described as 'a beautiful princess, as fresh as the dawn and sparkling with life'. She was a woman of wide-ranging talents – she spoke several languages, and was artistic, musically gifted and a great opera-lover.

She also enjoyed sports and was very fond of dogs and horses. Queen Marie-Henriette was active in the social field, too – an area that has traditionally been the preserve of Belgium's queens.

Her life, and that of her husband, was saddened by the premature death of their only son, Prince Leopold.

Heinrich von Angeli, *Queen Marie-Henriette, née the Archduchess of Austria*, 1870, oil on canvas.
Blue Drawing Room

ALBERT I,
KING FROM 1909 TO 1934

Albert I's greatest objective was actually the pursuit of peace. His primary goal during the First World War was to maintain Belgian independence and control over its territory. He worked hard to restore peaceful relations between the nations of Europe.

After the war, Albert realized the importance of reducing internal tensions. The King and the government also promised to introduce the single-vote universal suffrage

Leo Malempre, *Prince Albert at the Age of Seven*, 1882, oil on canvas.
Goya Room

Anonymous, *King Albert I*, undated, oil on canvas.
Blue Drawing Room

Albert, the youngest son of the Count of Flanders, succeeded his uncle as King of the Belgians, although his grooming for that role did not begin until the age of 16. He had a broad range of interests and travelled to the United States and Canada. His social concerns led him to criticize the colonial system in the Congo during a visit there.

Even though he has gone down in history as the 'Soldier-King',

and to introduce Dutch as the primary language of higher education in Flanders, although this was not realized until the 1930s.

King Albert died in a mountain-

eering accident in 1934 in Marche-les-Dames.

Fernand de Montigny, *Queen Elisabeth*, 1918,
pencil drawing.
Blue Drawing Room

Charles Samuel, *Queen Elisabeth,
née Duchess in Bavaria*, 1908, marble.
Ceremonial Vestibule

Queen Elisabeth's cultural and
scientific interests led to a number
of important initiatives and founda-
tions, including the Egyptological
Foundation, the Medical Foundation and the International Music
Competition that bear her name.
The Queen herself was a passionate
violinist and a gifted sculptor.

The first years of King Leopold III's reign were overshadowed by an economic crisis and the associated internal tensions. The climate elsewhere in Europe was equally troubled. Against this background, the King argued in favour of a better defence – not only to protect the country against possible invasion, but also to command respect from neighbouring countries, thereby promoting peace. Belgium decided to pursue a policy of neutrality, for which it sought support from other nearby neutral countries, such as the Netherlands.

Despite the fact that King and government adopted this policy, another war seemed inevitable. In May 1940, Belgium resisted the German invasion for 18 days, before Leopold decided to capitulate to avoid unnecessary further bloodshed.

Rather than fleeing abroad with the government, he chose to remain in Belgium as a prisoner-of-war, to share the fate of his soldiers. This decision sparked a conflict that was to split the country after the war. In 1941, six years after the death of Queen Astrid, he remarried Mary-Lilian Baels.

Liberation was followed by a bitter argument – the 'Royal Issue' – concerning the King's stance during the occupation. This led in 1951 to his abdication. Later Leopold devoted himself to the exploration and study of nature in Africa, Latin America and the Far East, picking up where he had left off as Duke of Brabant, when he and Princess Astrid had travelled widely.

Roger Trente, *King Leopold III*, 1993, oil on canvas.
'Il Pensieroso' Room

The Allies liberated Belgium in September 1944, but Leopold III remained abroad – a prisoner of the Germans. He was freed by the US Army in 1945, but domestic opposition to his return was so intense that he had to settle temporarily in Switzerland. During his absence, his brother Charles became acting head of state with the title Prince Regent. In this way, the Prince ensured the dynasty's continuity until the King returned in 1950. He subsequently withdrew from public life and settled in Raversijde, near Ostend, where he worked as an artist under the name 'Karel Van Vlaanderen'.

The spontaneity, friendliness and simplicity of Princess Astrid of Sweden won the hearts of the Belgian people. She pushed her pram through the park and joined the crowds with the young Joséphine-Charlotte to watch Prince Leopold parading through the streets.

When the country was hit by the economic crisis, Queen Astrid organized what came to be known as the 'Appeal to the Nation' in 1935, in which she called on the people to show solidarity and generosity towards the needy. She was killed on 29 August that same year in a car accident at Küssnacht, in Switzerland.

J. Bernhard Osterman, *Queen Astrid, c.* 1935, oil on canvas.
'Il Pensieroso' Room

Prince Charles, General Eisenhower and their staffs in the Flemish Hall of the Royal Palace in Brussels, 9 November 1944 (photo: Buyle)

Anne Rutten, *King Baudouin*, 1976, oil on canvas.
Blue Drawing Room

Baudouin was only 20 years old when he was crowned King of a country in the throes of social, economic and communal unrest. Fortunately, the world economy was beginning to prosper, which helped improve the situation in Belgium considerably. Meanwhile, the 1958 World Exhibition or 'Expo' in Brussels looked forward with great confidence to a modern world of technological progress and international collaboration.

Whatever the difficulties that arose, King Baudouin always attempted to solve them in a spirit of consensus and consultation. This applied, for instance, to moves towards independence for the Congo.

The King was also in favour of rapprochement between the countries of Europe and the growing importance of NATO. A large part of Belgium's armed forces is now designed to serve under NATO command. During King Baudouin's long reign, Belgium evolved from a unitary into a federal state – a process in which the King took a close interest, appealing to his compatriots to respect and understand one another.

He was deeply concerned about the more vulnerable members of society. It was typical of him to ask that no personal gifts be offered during the celebration of his Silver Jubilee. Financial donations gave birth to the King Baudouin Foundation, which initiates and supports projects designed to improve the living conditions of the Belgians.

King Baudouin died suddenly on 31 July 1993 in Motril in Spain.

Anne Rutten, *Queen Fabiola, née Mora y Aragón,*
1976, oil on canvas.
Blue Drawing Room

King Baudouin and Queen Fabiola were never blessed with offspring, which may partially explain their tireless interest in children and the most vulnerable members of society. A Social Section was added to the Queen's Secretarial Department to help them. Especially noteworthy was the Queen's contribution in the early 1990s to the Summit for the Economic Advancement of Rural Women and the International Steering Committee set up to pursue the same goal. Today, she is the Honorary Chairwoman of the King Baudouin Foundation.

Queen Fabiola has always taken a keen interest in art and culture. Since the death of Queen Elisabeth, she has been the Patron of the Queen Elisabeth International Music Competition and its Honorary Chairwoman. The contest has an international reputation and enthrals many Belgians throughout the weeks over which it unfolds.

Following the death of King Baudouin, Queen Fabiola took up residence at Stuyvenberg, on the royal estate of Laeken.

Albert was born on 6 June 1934 at the chateau of Stuyvenberg in Brussels. The son of King Leopold III and Queen Astrid, the title 'Prince of Liège' was bestowed on him at birth.

Prince Albert married Donna Paola Ruffo di Calabria, a descendant of an Italian princely family, on 2 July 1959. King Albert II and Queen Paola have three children: Prince Philippe, Princess Astrid and Prince Laurent.

In 1962 Prince Albert became Honorary President of the Belgian Foreign Trade Board. In the ensuing years, he presided over more than a hundred economic missions all over the world and visited many Belgian exporting firms. The Prince was also president of the General Council of the Caisse Générale d'Epargne et de Retraite from 1954 and President of the Belgian Red Cross from 1958.

Following the death of his brother, King Baudouin, Prince Albert was sworn in as the sixth King of the Belgians on 9 August 1993 before the Joint Houses of the Belgian Parliament. Right from the beginning of their reign, King Albert and Queen Paola have been in close contact with the Belgian people. The royal couple regularly visit every corner of the country and are interested in all aspects of society. Having signed the new Constitution creating a federal state on 17 February 1994, the King visited the Parliaments of the Communities and Regions. He has also participated in a variety of regional and community festivities.

At his daily audiences in the Palace in Brussels, the King meets representatives of the political, economic, social, cultural and sporting worlds, from both Belgium and abroad.

He also engages in many other activities – in every sector and every part of the country – that keep him up to date with the people's everyday concerns.

And as commander of the armed forces, the King holds the joint ranks of General and Admiral. He takes a close interest in military operations.

Dirk Braeckman (*1958), *Portrait of King Albert II, Portrait of Queen Paola and Four Accompanying Photographs*, 2002, silver gelatine print on aluminium in aluminium frames.
Sekhmet Room.
'The series of six photographs functions for Dirk Braeckman... as a unity. The royal portraits enter into an effortless dialogue with the abstracted, figurative images, further adding to the meanings of the multiple layers' (from the brochure published by the Belgian Buildings Authority on the presentation of the three contemporary art projects on 24 October 2002). The presence of the hieratic sculpture of the Egyptian goddess Sekhmet intensifies the overall atmosphere.

Queen Paola helps the King to perform his duties as head of state: visiting institutions, maintaining contact with the people, attending ceremonies in Belgium and abroad, going on state visits, receiving representatives of various groups in society and a great many other cultural and social activities. The Queen has developed her own activities in the social and cultural fields. She is a regular visitor – on her own initiative or by invitation – to social and healthcare institutions all over the country and takes a particular interest in young people in need. The Foundation that carries her name supports original educational projects. Queen Paola is also very concerned with the development and support of the arts – especially painting – as witnessed by her presence at important exhibitions both in Belgium and abroad. She is particularly devoted to the conservation of Belgium's cultural heritage.

Three contemporary art projects were unveiled in the Royal Palace in October 2002 on the initiative of the Queen and with the collaboration of the Belgian Buildings Authority. They feature the work of the photographer Dirk Braeckman, the painter Marthe Wéry and the all-round artist Jan Fabre. The three were selected by an arts advisory panel set up by the Queen and their work was designed and executed in and for the Palace. This bold but highly successful move will undoubtedly be followed by further projects by contemporary Belgian artists at the Palace.

Queen Paola is patron of 15 societies and grants her temporary Royal Patronage to a further 20 or so events every year. She keeps up an extensive correspondence with the country's citizens, not least with people in need who turn to her for assistance and mediation.

The Dance, tapestry after a cartoon by Francisco de Goya, 19th century, Royal Manufactory of St Barbara in Madrid. Goya Room. The tapestry was a gift of Queen Isabella II of Spain to King Leopold I.

The King of Belgium lives in the Belvédère, in the royal estate of Laeken, but comes to the Palace in Brussels every day, as it is here that he performs his duties as head of state. The Royal Palace is his official residence and office. Foreign heads of state are recieved here during their state visits to Belgium.

The Palace in Brussels belongs to the Belgian State, which provides the building and most of its contents as the King's official residence. As owner, it is also largely responsible for maintaining the complex.

Léon-Charles Cardon, *Dawn*,
ceiling paintings from the Long Gallery

Jean-Antoine Grosseau,
clock with posy of mechanical flowers, *c.*1830,
gilded bronze.
Leopold I Room

George Dawe, *Prince Leopold of Saxe-Coburg, c.*1817,
oil on canvas.
Leopold I Room

The Royal Palace stands on Coudenberg Hill – the site of the former residence of the Dukes of Brabant and Burgundy, and later of the Spanish and Austrian governors of the Southern Netherlands. The old palace was destroyed by fire in 1731 and it was not until half a century later that a new district of Brussels was constructed on the site in the neo-classical style. Four imposing blocks of houses were built in the 1780s on what is now the Place des Palais. Although they were detached, they shared the same sober, classical-style façades. Their occupants included the Austrian Minister Plenipotentiary and his Chancery for State and War. The decoration of several of the halls in the Royal Palace – the Empire Room and the White Drawing 29 Rooms – still dates largely from that period.

The Large White Drawing Room, late Austrian Period (1780s)

During the reign of William I, King of the Netherlands (1815–30), the two mansions in the middle were linked by a colonnade and extended at the rear, creating the buildings around what is now the Ceremonial Courtyard on the left. The staterooms and reception rooms were located along the northern façade. The Royal Family's private quarters and the audience chambers were built to the rear – the King's apartments to the south, the Queen's quarters to the east and the audience chambers to the west.

King William resided in both The Hague and Brussels, though his time in the latter cannot have been very comfortable, as work continued on the Palace throughout his reign. With the exception of one or two details, the Large Anteroom is a faithful record of that particular

stage of construction. The floor and southern end of the Empire Room also date from that period, when the hall was extended.

The Ceremonial Courtyard, built at the order of William I, King of the Netherlands (1815–30)

François Rude, *Navigation*, detail from the frieze. Large Anteroom

Arthur William Devis, *Allegory of the Death
of Princess Charlotte of Wales
on 6 November 1817*, c. 1818,
oil on canvas.
Louis XVI Room

King Leopold I moved into the new Palace in 1831. He ordered few changes, although, at the urging of his son and successor Leopold, he did approve plans for the building's extension. Work did not actually begin, however, until shortly before his death in 1865.

The Royal Palace took on its current, grandiose appearance under Leopold II. It was at this point that the Grand Staircase, the Throne Room, the Marble Room and the Long Gallery around the Brabant Courtyard were built and furnished. Several surviving areas, including the Venice Staircase and 'Il Pensieroso' Room, were harmonized with the rest of the building. Alphonse Balat (1818–1895) drew up the plans for the new constructions. The façade in the classical, Louis XVI style and the Hall of Mirrors were designed by Henri Maquet (1839–1909). Thomas Vinçotte (1850–1925) sculpted *Belgium between Agriculture and Industry*

– an allegory of Flanders and Wallonia – for the pediment of the principal façade.

The work had not been finished when Leopold II died in December 1909. It was completed in a more sober manner under Albert I. The Palace has since remained more or less unchanged, apart from periodic restoration. The King has lived in Laeken since 1935. The move coincided with the rise of the motorcar, which enabled the monarch to commute easily between Laeken and Brussels. The Royal Palace, originally the King's winter residence, thus became his 'office'.

An interesting new phase in the building's history began in 2002 with the introduction of contemporary art.

Motif in the parquet floor of the Throne Room

Following the success of the one-off opening of the Palace in 1965 as part of a major exhibition devoted to Leopold I and his time, King Baudouin decided to open the Palace to the public every summer. Visitors enter the palace by the same route that foreign diplomats take during the ceremonial presentation of their credentials to the King.

Seven paintings by Marthe Wéry (*1930) in a
ground-floor space off the Ceremonial Courtyard,
2002.
'Marthe Wéry's work testifies to her unwavering
desire to express unfathomable motivations and
experiences in colour and form, in an abstract, fun-
damental manner and using a variety of supports
in the context of a specific exhibition space' (from:
Marthe Wéry, exhibition catalogue Museum
Dhondt-Dhaenens, Deurle, 1995).

Alphonse Balat designed this majestic space, with its lovely proportions and tranquil atmosphere, for Leopold II. The pale stone of the walls and columns, the white marble of the broad staircase, the green marble of the banister, the gilding, the mirrors and windows, and the marble statue of Minerva form a bright and harmonious ensemble.

The busts in the Ceremonial Vestibule are portraits of Belgian Kings and Queens. There are also painted portraits of Leopold I (ill. p. 8) and Prince Leopold, Duke of Brabant (ill. p. 14).

Jean-Louis van Geel, *The Dutch Lion and Two Figures Representing the Low Countries,* detail from the frieze

François Rude, *Two Genii Pointing Out the Low Countries on the Globe,* detail from the frieze

The Large Anteroom dates from the period of Dutch rule, when the Northern and Southern Netherlands (modern Holland and Belgium) were united after the Battle of Waterloo to form the Kingdom of the Netherlands, ruled by King William I (1815–30). The frieze running around the room illustrates the political background to unification.

The allegorical figures in the frieze show the nation's four principal economic activities and the four pillars of effective rule. The bas-reliefs were sculpted by the Frenchman François Rude (1784–1855) and by

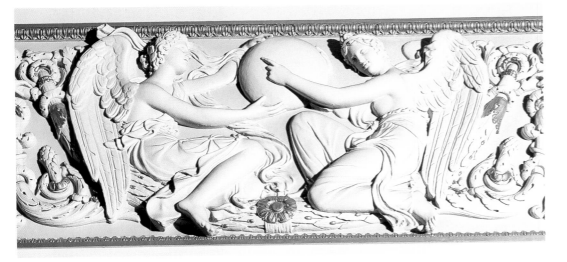

Jean-Louis van Geel (1787–1852) of
Mechelen. Rude was responsible for
the images of Commerce, Navigation, Plenty and Prudence, and for
the two figures pointing out the
Low Countries on a globe. Van Geel
sculpted Industry, Agriculture, the
Armed Forces and Peace. He also
produced the image of the unification of the Southern and Northern
Netherlands above the doorway
to the Grand Staircase. This relief
contains the only example of the
Dutch Lion (with sword and quiver
of arrows) to have survived in the
Palace.

The room contains several fine
portraits. The pendant portraits of
Prince Leopold (the later Leopold I)
and his first wife, Princess Charlotte
of Wales, are by the English artist
George Dawe. There are also por-
traits of Leopold I's parents – Duke
Franz of Saxe-Coburg and Augusta
Reuss-Ebersdorf – and those of
Queen Victoria – Edward, Duke of
Kent, and Victoria of Saxe-Coburg,
who was Leopold I's sister.

George Dawe, *Princess Charlotte of Wales, c.* 1817,
oil on canvas

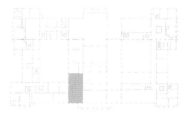

During the Austrian period, before the respective mansions were joined together to form a single palace, this chamber was used as a ballroom by the Minister Plenipotentiary, who lived in the house. The gilt decorations and bas-reliefs with angels dancing and playing musical instruments testify to the refined taste and lifestyle of the upper echelons of society towards the end of the *ancien régime.* William I had the room enlarged. The female figures above the mirrors (the work of Jean-Louis van Geel), the parquet flooring in oak and mahogany, the clock and the chandeliers date from this period. The Shah of Persia presented the marvellous Kirman carpet to King Leopold II during his state visit to Belgium around 1900.

The Empire Room was frequently used for concerts, balls and other ceremonial events, including the civil marriage of King Albert II and Queen Paola in 1959. It is also here that foreign ambassadors are received when they come to present their credentials to the King, and where the Court holds its New Year receptions for the European Community, NATO and SHAPE. When Prince Philippe was married in December 1999, the reception was held in the Empire Room.

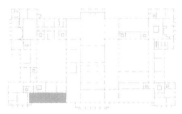

Like the Empire Room, these drawing rooms belong to the oldest
section of the Palace. Their late
18th-century decoration has survived in good condition. The Italian-
inspired grotesques in the Large
White Drawing Room (ill. p. 28–29)
are brilliant pieces of wood-carving,
while the clock on the mantelpiece
dates from the time of William I.

The Empire-style seating in both
rooms was a wedding gift from
King Louis-Philippe of France to his
daughter, Queen Louise-Marie, and
King Leopold I. The furniture still
has its original Beauvais tapestry
covers. Exceptional chairs like this
are, of course, only used by the King
on very special occasions.

The portraits in the Small White
Drawing Room show Queen
Louise-Marie and her parents,
King Louis-Philippe of France and
Marie-Amélie de Bourbon. The two
charming ladies with a corsage of
red roses are the sisters Stephanie
and Maria von Hohenzollern-
Sigmaringen. Stephanie was the
wife of King Pedro V of Portugal,
while Maria was married to
Philippe, Count of Flanders,
Leopold II's brother. Leopold II
had no direct descendants, and so
he was succeeded by the son of the
Count and Countess of Flanders –
King Albert I.

In the Large White Drawing
Room, the visitor's eye is drawn
irresistibly to the state portraits
of Leopold I and Louise-Marie

(ill. p. 12–13). It is here that the King
grants audiences to newly appointed
ambassadors.

Edouard Dubufe, *Louis-Philippe, King of France,
Duke of Orléans*, 1849, oil on canvas.
Small White Drawing Room

Covers of the seats in the Large White Drawing
Room, Beauvais tapestry-work,
first half 19th century, detail

Charles-François Jalabert, *Marie-Amélie de Bourbon,
Princess of the Two Sicilies, wife of Louis-Philippe*, 1882,
oil on canvas.
Small White Drawing Room

Joseph Leroy, *Queen Louise-Marie,
née Princess of Orléans*, 1850, pastel.
Small White Drawing Room

This part of the Palace was developed in the second half of the 19th century. Jean-Baptiste van

Moer painted the murals of the Venice Staircase in 1867.

Venice Staircase with murals by Jean-Baptiste van Moer

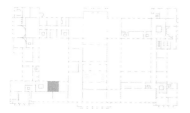

This room takes its name from the tapestries *The Dance* (ill. p. 24) and *The Blind Man*, which were woven in Madrid after designs by Francisco de Goya. Queen Isabella II of Spain had new versions made of several Goya tapestries from her collection as gifts for Leopold I.

The two gilt Empire chairs were made for Napoleon Bonaparte and Joséphine de Beauharnais in the early 19th century. In 1795 the Southern Netherlands were annexed by France. Napoleon visited his Belgian departments several times after coming to power in 1799. He had the chateau at Laeken refurbished at government expense as his *pied-à-*

terre in the region. After the defeat of Napoleon, the furniture left in the chateau became the property of the new state, which offered it to the King, who used Laeken in the summer and the Palace in Brussels in the winter. The porcelain *jardinières* in this room date from William I's time.

Blind Man, tapestry after a cartoon c. 1789 by Francisco de Goya, Royal Manufactory of St Barbara in Madrid

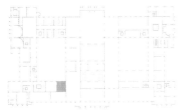

Much of what you see here originally belonged to the private apartments of Queen Louise-Marie in
Laeken. Several pieces had great
emotional importance to her because of the memories they evoked:
a watercolour showing a room in a
royal residence in France, another

depicting the chateau at Neuilly where she spent part of her youth, a pastel portrait believed to be of her governess Madame Angelet, a gouache portrait of her brother François d'Orléans and a watercolour of her daughter, Princess Charlotte, as a baby. There is a particularly moving marble bust of her first child, Prince Louis-Philippe of Belgium, who died at the age of one. The fine head was made by Willem Geefs.

Queen Louise-Marie also had several portraits of the young Leopold I and one of Princess Charlotte of Wales, Leopold's first wife (drawing in coloured chalk by Thomas Lawrence, 1817), which hung in her private quarters.

The clock with the posy of artificial flowers beneath a bell jar is an ingenious mechanical piece that William I bought in 1830 at the Brussels Industrial Exhibition (ill. p. 26). The clock mechanism causes the flowers to bloom. Unfortunately, the Palace no longer employs a clock-winder and so time here now stands still.

Prince Leopold of Saxe-Coburg at the Age of Five, 1795, pastel. There is a verse on the back for his grandmother, the Duchess of Saxe-Coburg

Prince Leopold of Saxe-Coburg, *Schloss Rosenau*, 1811. This small pencil drawing by Prince Leopold shows the castle of his grandmother, the Duchess of Saxe-Coburg

Ange Ottoz
after Franz-Xaver
Winterhalter,
Queen Louise, 1845,
oil on canvas

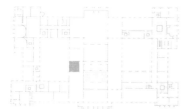

Between the Empire Room and the Throne Room there are three chambers that date from William I's time: two antechambers and an audience chamber (now the Marshals' Room).

The Louis XVI Room is actually more of a 'Leopold I Room'. Apart from portraits of his parents and his children (all except Louis-Philippe, who died as a baby), it contains several paintings from his personal collection and an allegorical image of his first wife (ill. p. 32 and 39). It may not be immediately obvious, and it certainly does not spoil the effect, but the furniture and objects in this room do not form a true ensemble. They were produced in a variety of eras and locations, yet they complement one another nicely.

The harp and the music stand almost certainly belonged to Queen Louise-Marie. The Louis XVI folding chair (final quarter 18th century) came from Louis XVI's room in the chateau of Compiègne and found its way to Laeken via Napoleon Bonaparte before being transferred to Brussels. The chair was restored in the 1960s, when it was re-covered with fabric woven after the original design. The Klems piano originally belonged to the Count and Countess of Flanders, King Albert I's parents, to whom it had been given as a wedding present in 1867. It was kept in their palace on the Place Royale. It is a fine piece made of ebony inlaid with copper, mother of pearl, rosewood and tortoise shell.

Willem Geefs, *Princess Charlotte of Belgium at the Age of Two*, marble

The central room of the three was originally a guardroom, before being converted into a dining room for court dignitaries ('marshals'). This function is recalled by the table with its early 19th-century crockery and cutlery. The marshals' mealtimes will, however, have been simpler than this. The crockery displayed here was only used at the royal table. Leopold I brought back the silverware and the thistle-shaped crystal glasses from England and Scotland. The porcelain was made around 1830 by Faber of Brussels. Each plate is decorated with a different bird.

Four of the many Empire-style armchairs were kept at Laeken until 1815. They belonged to the furniture used by Napoleon Bonaparte and Joséphine de Beauharnais.

The room now contains many painted and sculpted portraits of members of the Royal Family (ill. p. 15–17 and 20–21).

School of Rubens, *The Stoning of St Stephen*, 17th century, oil on canvas
Louis XVI Room

Joseph Damien and Anne Rutten, *Queen Astrid, née Princess of Sweden*, 1936, oil on canvas

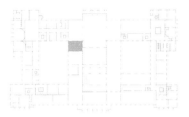

This room – originally William I's audience chamber and later the marshals' drawing room – leads directly into the Throne Room. Before you enter the latter, however, you should take time to look at several interesting portraits of members of the Royal Family, including Prince Philippe, Count of Flanders. The second son of Leopold I, he was King Albert I's father. The man in the white uniform is Prince Friedrich-Josias of Saxe-Coburg, Leopold I's great-uncle and a field marshal in the Austrian army. The younger man with the startling blue eyes is Archduke Maximilian of Austria, the husband of Princess Charlotte and son-in-law of Leopold I. Maximilian was made Emperor of Mexico in 1864, but was executed in 1867 by Juárez's rebels. Charlotte went insane and spent the rest of her life, until 1927, at the chateau of Bouchout in Meise.

Jan Portaels, *Prince Philippe, Count of Flanders,* 1858, oil on canvas

Gustaf Wappers, *Queen Louise-Marie*, c. 1835, oil on canvas.

Queen Louise-Marie wore the ermine cloak during a state visit to Britain, where court costume of this type was the norm. Royal attributes such as thrones, sceptres, crowns and ermine date from the period before the French Revolution, usually referred to as the *ancien régime*. They refer to the omnipotence of the ruler. Since its creation in 1830, Belgium has been a constitutional monarchy and symbols of this kind are not used here. They would not be in keeping with the reality of the Belgian state. You will not, for instance, find a throne in the Palace, even though the next chamber is called the 'Throne Room'

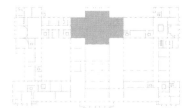

The Throne Room offers a clear insight into the grandiose vision of Leopold II. This part of the Palace and the rooms you will visit in a moment were constructed during his reign. You are now in the rear part of the complex, located between the two wings. The Grand Staircase and the Large Anteroom are also here.

The bas-reliefs are the work of various sculptors, amongst them Auguste Rodin (1840–1917) and Thomas Vinçotte (1850–1925). Rodin worked on the decoration of the central part of the room, where each relief shows two economic activities carried out in the various Belgian provinces: hunting (Luxembourg) and heavy industry (Liège), fishing (West Flanders) and textiles (East Flanders), overseas trade (Antwerp) and cattle husbandry (Limbourg), mining (Hainaut) and quarrying (Namur). Only the province of Brabant is missing, although it is implicitly included by the fact that the Palace is located on Brabant soil. Above the doors on either side of the Throne Room, we see personifications of the rivers Meuse (female) and Scheldt (male), symbolizing Wallonia and Flanders. These bas-reliefs were made by Vinçotte.

Everything in this room – the parquet flooring in oak and exotic woods, the fine bronze chandeliers and the gilt decorations – evokes a sense of royal prestige and deco-

rum. This is precisely how Leopold II wished it to look.

The Throne Room is used to hold important receptions, such as the one given for the Government at New Year, and for the Palace and Christmas concerts. The King Baudouin Prize and the triennial Prize for Literature in Dutch are also presented here. In December 1960 the room was used for the civil marriage of King Baudouin and Queen Fabiola.

Auguste Rodin, *Hunting and Heavy Industry.*
The bas-relief is an allegory of the provinces
of Luxembourg and Liège

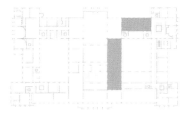

The abundant use of green marble, the monumental atmosphere and the equestrian portraits above the fireplaces give the Marble Room a very masculine feel.

The artist Louis Gallait (1810–1887), who was very famous in his day, painted Godefroi de Bouillon and Emperor Charles V – a pair of equestrian portraits that refer to the historic roots of the young Belgian state.

The Marble Room takes you back briefly into the Throne Room and from there into the Long Gallery. The latter remains the ideal space for receptions and dinners with a large number of guests, as occurred in December 1999, on the occasion of Prince Philippe's wedding. The furniture comprises the original pieces produced in the latter half of the 19th century for this specific location. Léon-Charles Cardon's ceiling paintings show Dawn (ill. p. 25), Morning, Daytime and Twilight. The artist drew inspiration from the work of the French court painters Charles Le Brun and Louis-Jacques Durameau in the Louvre and at Versailles.

Decoration of the doors in the Throne Room

The Long Gallery

The Long Gallery runs from the Throne Room past the Grand Staircase to the front of the Palace, where it leads into a small drawing room. The latter is known as 'Il Pensieroso' Room, because of the clock it contains, with a bronze reproduction of Michelangelo's *Il Pensieroso* (The Thinker). It contains a portrait of King Leopold III and one of Queen Astrid (ill. pp. 18–19). The room is used as a chapel of mourning when a member of the Royal Family dies.

'Il Pensieroso' Room adjoins the Large Anteroom and the Hall of Mirrors – an unfinished stateroom from the time of Leopold II.

The Hall of Mirrors was constructed in the early years of the 20th century. The King evidently intended to create a 'Congo Room', as we see from the map of Africa in the pediment above the fireplace. The luxuriant floral motifs in the decoration also refer to exotic and tropical regions. The walls, meanwhile, are decorated with an abundance of marble and copper rather than gold, as the Congo produced copper ore on a large scale.

Shortage of funds more or less put an end to building work on King Leopold II's death in 1909. Albert I completed the room, although not according to the original plan. Mirrors were installed on the walls rather than allegories of the 'dark continent', and the ceiling was not decorated. In 2002, the artist

Jan Fabre (*1958) turned the unfinished ceiling into a glittering deep-green and blue sea of jewel beetle wing-cases, which also cover one of the three impressive chandeliers. The room is also frequently used for festive receptions.

It is here that your visit to the Royal Palace comes to an end.

Heaven of Delight, detail. The barrel vault, the semicircular tympana at either end and the central chandelier in the Hall of Mirrors are set with the wing-cases of around 1.4 million Thai jewel beetles. A team of 29 young artists and restorers completed the painstaking task under Jan Fabre's supervision

Clock known as *Il Pensieroso*,
inspired by Michelangelo's Medici Tomb
in Florence, black and gilded bronze.
'Il Pensieroso' Room

The following bibliography is intended to assist anyone wishing to learn more about the Royal Palace's history, architecture and art collection.

Cover of the fireguard in the Large White Drawing Room, Beauvais tapestry, first half 19th century

André Molitor, Gustaaf Janssens, Martine Vermeire, Guy de Greef, *The Royal Palace in Brussels,* in the Musea Nostra series (series editors Jean-Marie Duvosquel and Valentin Vermeersch), Crédit Communal/Ludion, Ghent 1993. This publication was the principal source for the new Ludion Guide.

Exposition nationale Léopold Ier et son règne organisée par le Gouvernement à l'occasion du centième anniversaire de la mort du Roi, exhibition catalogue, Royal Palace, Brussels, Archives générales du Royaume, Brussels 1965.

Liane Ranieri, *Léopold II, urbaniste,* Hayez, Brussels 1973.

Richard Vandendaele et al., *Poelaert et son temps,* exhibition catalogue (Institut Supérieur d'Architecture Victor Horta), City of Brussels/Crédit Communal de Belgique, Brussels 1980.

Nous, Roi des Belges, 150 ans de monarchie constitutionnelle, exhibition catalogue, Royal Palace, Brussels, Crédit Communal de Belgique, Brussels 1981.

Nos reines, exhibition catalogue, Musée Royal de l'Armée et d'Histoire Militaire, Brussels 1982.

Herman Balthazar and Jean Stengers (eds.), *Dynastie et culture en Belgique,* Fonds Mercator, Antwerp 1990.

Anne van Ypersele de Strihou, 'Auguste Rodin au Palais de Bruxelles', in *Maisons d'hier et d'aujourd'hui,* 1990, 86, pp. 59–68.

Anne van Ypersele de Strihou, 'La décoration de la Grande Galerie du Palais royal de Bruxelles, de Louis XIV à Léopold II', in *Maisons d'hier et d'aujourd'hui,* 1993, 98, pp. 10–32.

Marthe Wéry, exhibition catalogue, Museum Dhondt-Dhaenens, Deurle 1995.

Piet Lombaerde and Ronny Gobyn, *Leopold II Roi-Bâtisseur,* Pandora, Ghent 1995.

Henri van Daele, *Six Rois,* Editions Racine, Brussels 1995.

Henri van Daele, *Six Reines,* Editions Racine, Brussels 1996.

Brochure published by the Belgian Buildings Authority on the presentation of three contemporary art projects on 24 October 2002.

Dirk Braeckman, Stefan Hertmans, Roger H. Marijnissen, *Heaven of Delight – Jan Fabre, Royal Palace,* Brussels, Mercatorfonds, Antwerp 2002.

The Empire Room, detail (see p. 40)

We respectfully offer our gratitude
to Their Royal Majesties the King
and Queen. We also thank all those
who have provided their willing
assistance during the compilation
of this guide.

Photo credits
Dirk Braeckman: pp. 22–23
Bart Cloet: cover, pp. 25, 28, 30, 36, 47, 56, 59, 64
Hugo Maertens: pp. 8, 12, 13, 14, 16, 24, 27, 38, 39, 42, 43 left, 46, 48, 49, 52, 54, 55, 61
Dirk Pauwels: pp. 2, 34–35, 60
Luc Schrobiltgen: pp. 4, 6, 15, 17, 18, 19, 20, 21, 23, 26, 31, 32, 33, 37, 41, 43 right, 44, 45, 50, 51, 53, 58, 62, 63
Van Parys Media: p. 9

Pp. 20, 21, 53: cfr. A. Molitor, G. Janssens, M. Vermeire, G. de Greef, *The Royal Palace in Brussels,* Crédit Communal/ Ludion, Ghent 1993, pp. 120–121

© 2000–2003 Ludion Press Ghent-Amsterdam and Irene Smets
© 2003 Dirk Braeckman, Jan Fabre, Marthe Wéry
Translation: Ted Alkins, Heverlee
Design: Antoon De Vylder, Herentals
Typesetting: De Diamant Pers, Herentals
Colour separations and printing: Die Keure, Bruges
D/2000/6328/13
ISBN: 90-5544-296-8